Norman Macpherson

Notes on the Chapel, Crown and Other Ancient Buildings of King's College, Aberdeen

Norman Macpherson

Notes on the Chapel, Crown and Other Ancient Buildings of King's College, Aberdeen

ISBN/EAN: 9783337267391

Printed in Europe, USA, Canada, Australia, Japan

Cover: Foto ©Andreas Hilbeck / pixelio.de

More available books at **www.hansebooks.com**

NOTES
ON THE
CHAPEL, CROWN,
AND
OTHER ANCIENT BUILDINGS
OF
KING'S COLLEGE, ABERDEEN.

BY

NORMAN MACPHERSON, LL.D. Abd. et Edin., F.S.A.

(REPRINTED FROM ARCHÆOLOGIA SCOTICA.)

WITH SEVENTEEN PLATES (LIV.–LXX.)

EDINBURGH:
PRINTED BY NEILL AND COMPANY.
1889.

Note.—While examining the subject of Choir and Chancel Screen, I have become acquainted with many beautiful examples in England, and by the kind permission of the Publisher and the Artist, I have been able to add to the illustrations of this paper the very effective (post-Reformation) Screen at Croscombe, near Wells (Plate LXVIII.), which I first saw noticed in the *Magazine of Art* for last year.

ON THE CHAPEL AND ANCIENT BUILDINGS

OF

KING'S COLLEGE, ABERDEEN.

Not long ago I walked over the University buildings, new and old, at King's College, Aberdeen, with Principal Geddes. As we were parting, he remarked that some of the details I mentioned to him regarding the old parts of the structure seemed to him to possess an architectural and ecclesiological interest that made them worth putting permanently on record; and he suggested that I should do this before the memory of them passed away. Hence this paper, stating what I believe to have been some points of the history of the Chapel—or "Templum" as it was called in old writs, and of the "campanile" with its crown: these being all that remain of the original buildings erected by Bishop Elphinstone, except perhaps the round ivy-covered tower, now deprived of the spire added to it by Bishop Stewart. It marks the south-east corner of the College as it stood when first completed.

My connection with the University of Aberdeen may be said to be hereditary. It is more than a century since my father, Dr Hugh Macpherson, entered King's College as a student, where he afterwards became Professor of Greek and Sub-Principal. My maternal grandfather, Dr Roderick Macleod, was one of the Regents, forty years earlier, and after sixty-eight years ended his Professoriate as Principal. Many old traditions of the place were consequently known to my parents, and I can hardly distinguish between what I learnt from them and what I have picked up from books. Much that I first heard from them I have been able to corroborate from books.

I owe much to the old chroniclers, and cannot hope to rival either the beauty or expressiveness of their quaint language. What, for instance, can be better than this?—

"Ther is in this Universitie" of Aberdeen " a magnifick and illustrious

Colledge . . . . . called the King's Colledge, having a collegiat kirk and steeple, both of hewin stone curiouslie wrought and covered with lead: and the steeple hath within it an musicall harmonic of costlie and pleasant bells, and above the covering of leid a most curious and statlie work of hewin and corned stones, representing to the vieu of all beholders a brave pourtrait of the royall diademe."[1]

After this crown had stood for more than a century—the latter half of the period being little favourable to the preservation of ancient ecclesiastical edifices—we find, on 13th June 1620, very extensive repairs "ordanet," and *inter alia*, "Seventintlie, that the heid of the gryt Stepill sould be mendit in steane leid and tymer as the samen was abefoir."[2]

Before proceeding farther, it is well to quote the terms of the general instructions of 14th Sept. 1619 as to the "repairs of the haill edefeis,"—instructions which it would be well if all who venture to engage in such works would observe. They were to be repaired "with leid quhair leid was, sklaittis quhair sklaitt was, aik quhair aik was, fir quhair fir was, lyme quhair lyme was, heuine steane quhair heuine steane was."

The repairs, which were ordered, seem not to have been executed, for "this goodlie ornament was by an extraordinar tempest of stormie wind in the moneth of Februar 1633 throun doune, quherby both the roofes of tymber and lead and other adjacent works wer pitifullie crushed, and that Royall crown loosed to the great grieff of the Universitie." "Bot the crown was quicklie afterwards restored in a better forme and condition by the direction of Patrick Forbes of Corse, then Bishop of Aberdeen."[3]

Twice in the eighteenth, and also in the early part of the present century, the crown seems to have fallen into a dangerous state of disrepair; and again in 1860—when the charge of the University buildings was taken over by Government—the condition of the crown was found in need of immediate attention.

The chroniclers, with general consent, speak of the wonderful harmony and musical quality of the "Tunable" bells in the tower, which is said to

---

[1] Appendix to paper of representations to the king, dated 1634, *Fasti Aberdonenses*, p. 309.
[2] *Fasti Aberdonenses*, p. 283.
[3] Gordon's *Description of Aberdeen*, p. 23. The Magistrates of Aberdeen contributed out of the common good, and sanctioned also a local subscription; Burgh Records, 29th May 1633 and 6th Aug. 1634.

THE CROWN OF KINGS COLLEGE
AS RESTORED AFTER DESTRUCTION
IN 1633.

have been such that they might call the very stones to prayer by the sweetness of their melody,

"Quæ vel lapides dulcissima melodia ad sacra vocarent." [1]

We learn from the Register of the furnishings of the College prepared in 1542,[2] that there were five great bells in the Tower, named Trinitas, Maria, Michael, Gabriel, and Raphael.

Five small bells for striking the half hours, with a like number of iron hammers, two bells for daily use, besides three bells in the chapel.

Of the great bells we are told that "there were two of greater weight each than any in Scotland besyde,"[3] which we can readily believe from the measurement given of that named Trinitas, namely, 5 feet 5 inches.[4]

Though these great bells were probably in their place down to 1700, it is difficult not to suppose that by that time they had either been damaged, perhaps by the falling of the crown, or were considered too heavy to ring, for in that year Mons. Gelly, a French founder, offered, if the College would "breake doune the said bells and delyver to him the mettall," he would, "out of two parts of the said metall, cast for the College use five or six good and sufficient musicall bells." He demanded the remaining third part of the metal for himself.[5]

As it was "not possible to get the bells recasten so easily elsewhere," it was "resolved that for a tryall the two bells hingeing next to the eight houer bell be broken and that out of them he be allowed to cast one, ... and if this answer our expectation, then may we proceed ..... by piecemeale to brake doun the rest." How far Mons. Gelly ultimately proceeded we do not know. There remained till the present century bells so large that the college architect ordered them not to be used, but whether they were of the original five is not known. As they were condemned to silence, and the University was in great straits for want of money to complete repairs

---

[1] Strachani Panegyricus Inauguralis, 1631, p. 10.
[2] Fasti Aberdonenses, p. 571.   [3] Gordon, p. 23.
[4] Orem, Old Aberdeen, p. 169. He has also preserved the inscription on each of the bells :—
  (1) Trinitas—"Trinitate sacra fiat, hæc campana beata."
  (2) Maria—"Protege precor pia, quos convoco. Sancta Maria."
  (3) Michael—"En annuncio vobis novum gaudium, quod erit omni populo."
  (4) "Vocor Gabriel, Cantate Domino canticum novum bene. Psallite et vociferatione."
  (5) "Raphael Cantate Domino canticum novum bene. Psallite ei in vociferatione."
  Per Geo. Weyhevens MDXIX is inscribed on the three last. Bishop Elphinstone died 1514.
[5] Fasti Aberdonenses, p. 438.

and the new west front in 1823, the dismounted bells were sold, and the largest door of the tower being too small for their removal, the wall had to be broken for the purpose. I remember seeing inside the tower the comparatively fresh plaster where the broken part of the wall was built up.

There were still two bells in the tower when I was at College—the bell which rung the curfew[1] and for chapel services and the one known as "Clatter Vengeance." An inscription on the former shows that it was recast by Mons. Gelly in 1702.

"Clatter Vengeance" was certainly not one of the great bells. Before 1823 it hung in the tower at the south-east corner of the apse of the chapel.[2] The tower is shown in Gordon's drawing (Plate LV. fig. 2). The top of the tower is also seen in the view printed by Wilson[3] (Plate LXIV. fig. 1), and in Slezer's view.[4] Many a time have I rung "Clatter Vengeance" in my boyhood. It sent forth two very distinct sounds, according to different traditional modes of ringing it. The one was used to call the students to morning prayer and to lecture; the other—and every student knew it well—was only heard when the call was to "discipline." I cannot say that "Clatter Vengeance," by its *dulcissima melodia*, was calculated to charm the savage breast, much less call the stones to prayer, but it had rung out the hours for centuries at the corner of that chapel, and had been written of in prose and verse, and has, I understand, received an honoured place in the University Museum. It bears the following inscription:—

"JOHANNES BVRGERHVYS ME FECIT,
1699.
COLLEGIUM REGIUM ABERDONENSIS."

The "maxie" in the inscription is not creditable to a University bell.

There were belonging to the Church of *Sta Maria ad nives*, once the parish church of Old Aberdeen, which was annexed to the college, two bells known as Shoehtmadony and Skellat. They were of sufficient importance

---

[1] At nine o'clock, an hour for which one feels some sympathy when reading the College rule, "Mane hora quinta ad matinasbeii omnes omnes surgunto."—*Fasti Aberd.*, p. 228.

[2] It is possibly the bell referred to by Orem (p. 183) in the following passage:—"The timber lusses or little chambers at the east end of the College Chapel were built when the building of the said new work was built in which there is a bell that is rung at several hours both in the day and night time." The want of such a bell at an earlier period appears from the fact that on 14th October 1640 the Provost and Ballies "aggries to len" the "bell of the grammer schuill" to Dr Guild, "now primar to the Kings College, for the use of the said college wpoun his ticquat and for redelyverie of the same."—Extracts from Burgh Records, p. 243.

[3] Wilson's *Delineation of Aberdeen*. [4] Given in Gordon's *Description of Aberdeen*, Spald. Club Ed.

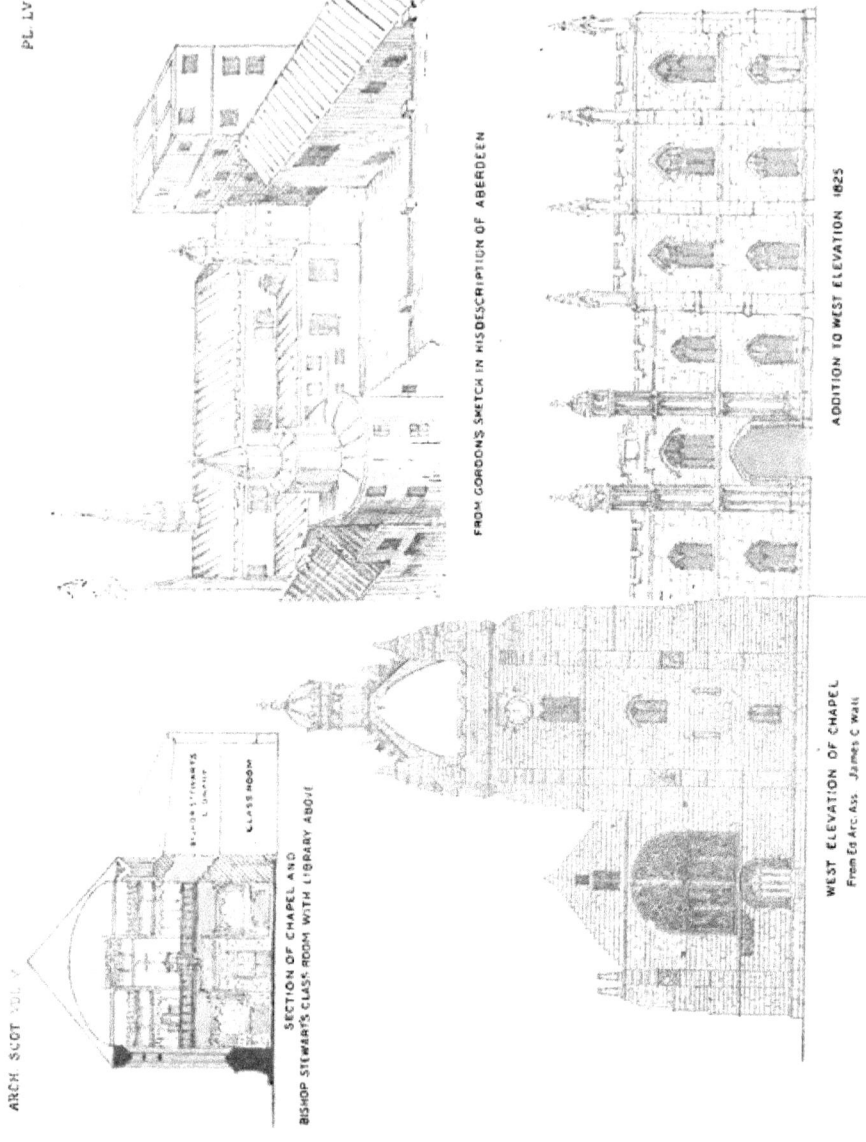

to have their transfer to that church recorded in a charter by the chapter of the Cathedral on the penult of Sept. 1503(5).[1]

I have read no attempt to identify the saints to whom these bells belonged. Some have suggested that we have in Shochtmadony notice of a bell of the Madonna. I have not observed any other example in Scotland of the Virgin being so designated. "Our Lady" is common enough. It may be said "the exception proves the rule," but I incline to think we have here a conveyance of a bell of St Modanus. There are two Scottish saints of that name mentioned in the *Aberdeen Breviary*. Bishop Forbes, in his *Kalendar*, tells us that in Auchmeddan, Pitmeden, and St Meddan of Fintry, near Aberdeen, we have local modifications of Modanus,—they are greater than the transposition of the *o* and *a*. "Shocht" I look upon as a precatory prefix, whether addressed to the saint or to the custodier of the bell. "Shog" or "Shoch" appear in many Scots words, always implying unsteady movement; and Jamieson in his *Dictionary* says, "Shog" means "to pull backwards and forwards."

As regards the other bell,—"Skellat,"—that was a common name for bells in early days, and no saint's name is here associated with it. Doubtless in the Scotch word *skelloch* as well as in the German "schellen" we have the same root, though Jamieson suggests a French origin; he says, "Skellat, a small bell. O. Fr. eschelette petite sonnette crecelle. We learn from Roquefort that it was used in monasteries for awaking the religious, and also for proclamations."

It seems to have been a general name applied to small bells—ecclesiastical and secular. The ecclesiastical skellats were sometimes highly ornate, sometimes perfectly simple, cast in bronze (fig. 2, next page) or even rudely hammered iron.[2]

Among secular bells the word came to be applied as the technical name for the bells used in burghs for making proclamations. The old Edinburgh Skellat, now in the Antiquarian Museum, is shown in next page. Dougal Graham, the ballad writer and historian of the '45, was "Skellat-bellman" of the City of Glasgow. The word does not seem to have applied to the bells carried at funerals, and we have notice that the "Deid-Bell" in Glasgow

---

[1] *Fasti Aberd.*, p. 47.
[2] See many engravings of such bells in *Scotland in Early Christian Times*, by Dr Joseph Anderson.

was not held by the Skellat-bellman. This distinction makes it not unlikely that the Skellat referred to in the gift to *St Maria ad nives* may have been the subject of a dispute two hundred years afterwards which is referred to by Orem.[1] "The present (1692) hand-bell belonged to the town being gifted by the deceast John Ross, sometime janitor in the King's College. But in 1702 this right was renounced in favor of the Minister and Kirk Session on the ground that the hand-bell which goeth before interments doth entirely belong to the Church."

 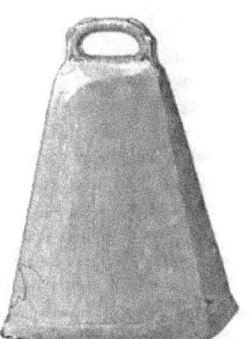

FIG. 1.—The Old Skellat Bell of Edinburgh.   FIG. 2.—St Fillan's Bell.

The College Chapel is on the north side of the quadrangle and of the tower with the Crown.

On the south wall of the chapel abutted the library, and what better support could a church have than learning? This part of the building was not completed by Bishop Elphinstone, nor even by his executor Bishop Dunbar, but by Bishop Stewart, who "built the Librarie hous and with a number of bookes furnisht the same, as also he built the jewell or charter house, and vestrie or Chapter house." Under the library were class-rooms.

---

[1] *History of Old Aberdeen*, p. 129.

These buildings are shown in Gordon's sketch (Plate LVI. fig. 2), from which it will be seen that they did not extend the whole length of the chapel, but left one large window to the west of the apse. They were low enough to give room above the almost flat roof for the small square-headed windows which still light the chapel on the south.

The entrance to the quadrangle is very different from the old and humble one (according to Jamieson's sketch), which had served good purpose in its day, for doubtless it aided Principal Anderson,[1] when he defended the College from the mob of men of the Mearns, who, after plundering the cathedral and robbing it of its lead, sought to do the same by the College. " Forti manu vim vi repellere nititur, audacem fortuna juvante, integra et intacta huc usque manent augusta musæum tecta."[2] The last occasion on which the College was defended was about 1770, when students still lived within its walls, and by means of the same gate.[3]

Over the gate at one time was a stone, with the royal arms vigorously sculptured on it,—probably the shield which is now seen on one of the buttresses of the south side of the chapel (Plate LXIV. fig. 2), where it was removed "some time ago," says Kennedy,[4] when the gate was taken down. That time we know was subsequent to 1725, when Orem[5] wrote, for, besides mentioning the "King's armorial coat above the entry gate," he enumerates the arms that were on the wall of the library built by Fraser, and the royal arms are not in his list, which was probably checked down to 1771.

The shield in question must have been substituted for an older one, for

---

[1] He was the last Principal before the Reformation, and was in 1569 deprived of his office for refusing to sign articles approving of the Confession of Faith.
[2] Descriptio, Ker, 1725, p. 17.
[3] Aberdeen was then but a small place, and its harbour small in proportion, and frequented by few vessels and of light burden. There used to be frequent "bickers" between the students and the younger sailors. After one of these contests, in which the sailors had the worst of it, the defeated party went the round of the shipping in port, and having gathered a strong reinforcement, gave chase to the students, who were quite unconscious of pursuit, on their way home, and they had hardly reached the College when the mob came in sight. They had just time to rush in, and shut and bar the gate. But sailors are eminently full of resource, and finding wood lying near where two new professors' houses were being built, they soon improvised a battering-ram, and were at the point of bringing it against the gate, when, lo! it opened voluntarily, and out walked Professor Gordon, who happened to be the hebdomadar, with his hat in his hand and his white hair falling on his shoulders, and implored the sailors to go home, and return next day, by which time he promised that the whole facts should be inquired into, and that every satisfaction that was due would certainly be given. Thereupon the sailors marched off with a cheer, and they were too busy to return next day for the promised satisfaction. I had the tale half a century ago from an eye-witness.
[4] Annals of Aberdeen, vol. ii. p. 397, published in 1818.
[5] Old Aberdeen, p. 40.

heralds tell us that it has various characteristics of date long subsequent to the time of Jac. IV., whose name is on it.

Douglas, professing to write in 1780, tells us, p. 161—"Several of the professors have manses without the gates, and two very handsome ones have lately been built adjoining to the west wall of the garden." These two still stand at the south-west angle of the College buildings, and no doubt it was when these were being built that the old gate was removed, leaving a considerable part of the west front open, as seen in the drawing of 1818[1] (Plate LXIV. fig. 1).

To the north of the gate, on the first buttress are **the arms of A. Stewart, archbishop of St Andrews; while on the second are the royal arms of James IV., and the date 1504; and on the north buttress of the chapel those of his Queen, Margaret Tudor.**

On the north side of the west door of the chapel is the inscription recording the commencement of the building in 1500, per "serenissimum et invictissimum . . . . . Jacobum IV. Regem." Little did Elphinstone then foresee the disaster of Flodden, which he felt so keenly that it is said he was never after seen to smile. Over the west door is a remarkable round-headed window of four lights, with a thick perpendicular mullion built up to the top of the arch, the upper part of the window on either side being filled with heavy cusped tracery. There are few examples of such heavy tracery **remaining in** Scotland. But the old engravings **of St** Giles's before its **first restoration (?)** show something similar. The **north** wall of the chapel **is divided into six** bays, five pierced with windows nearly equally large, while one is occupied by a doorway, **over which are** found again the arms **of the Archbishop.** One only **of the north windows is** round-headed like the **west window.** The others **are** pointed, and **all but that farthest east** have the same heavy mullion running up the centre to the top **of the arch.** This massive perpendicular mullion may be seen in **Flanders, as in** the large east window in the Cathedral of Liege (Plate LXVII.), **and in** the church of St Jacques in the same city. It is long since Principal Geddes directed attention to the Flemish character of some of the windows.[2]

The tracery of the windows of the apse and the windows next it, both north and south, is entirely different in character. It is modern, dating only from 1823. What it was before that date I do not know, farther

---

[1] Wilson's *Delineation of Aberdeen*. [2] "Local Aspects of the Fine Arts," *Phil. Soc. Abd.*, 1874.

CHAPEL AND TOWER, KING'S COLLEGE ABERDEEN UNIVERSITY.
Nº 2.

NORTH ELEVATION. (Sanctuary)

ought to be done now). The chapel seems to have consisted of four squares, two allotted to the nave and two to the choir, with the addition of the apse, the breadth being equal to the height of the walls, above which the roof was alcoved.

Half-way up the nave, on either side, was a door—one by which the members of the College entered from the quadrangle, the other by which those who died were borne out to their final resting-place in the cemetery of the College.

With regard to the other features of the nave, it must be remembered that **this was strictly a collegiate, not a parochial church, but yet** one in which it was provided that there should be public services. In proper parochial churches, even where there were a considerable number of clergy, the stalls were often arranged along the walls, and did not return across the **church, so that, where there was a choir screen with a loft above, it was** possible, by supporting the loft on open arches instead of a solid screen, to enable the people in the nave to have a full view of the services **at the high altar.** But when the church was attached to a convent or other collegiate establishment, and a larger number of stalls was required, they **were generally** returned across the church, and a doorway left in the centre.

When this was so, those in the nave could neither see nor well **hear the services in the** choir, and therefore special arrangements had to **be made for their benefit;** and these varied with the size of the church and the taste and skill **of the architect.** The plan more ordinarily adopted was this—The great crucifix, which in many churches hung from the roof, or from a rood beam, often highly ornamented, stretching from wall to wall, **came to be fixed on a gallery** above and to the west of the stalls, and on this gallery were placed an ambone, or perhaps two, from which the Epistle **and Gospel were read** to those in the nave.

Frequently the Host was exhibited from this gallery. It was not uncommon to have an altar upon it, and it was usual to have altars under it, at which those could worship who were strictly excluded from the portion of the chapel intended for the accommodation of the members of the Convent or College.

There have been fortunately preserved so much of the woodwork used in this part of King's College Chapel as—with the aid of the written record dated 1542, showing what altars were in the nave—to leave very few points to conjecture.

The breadth of the nave was divided into three portions, the centre

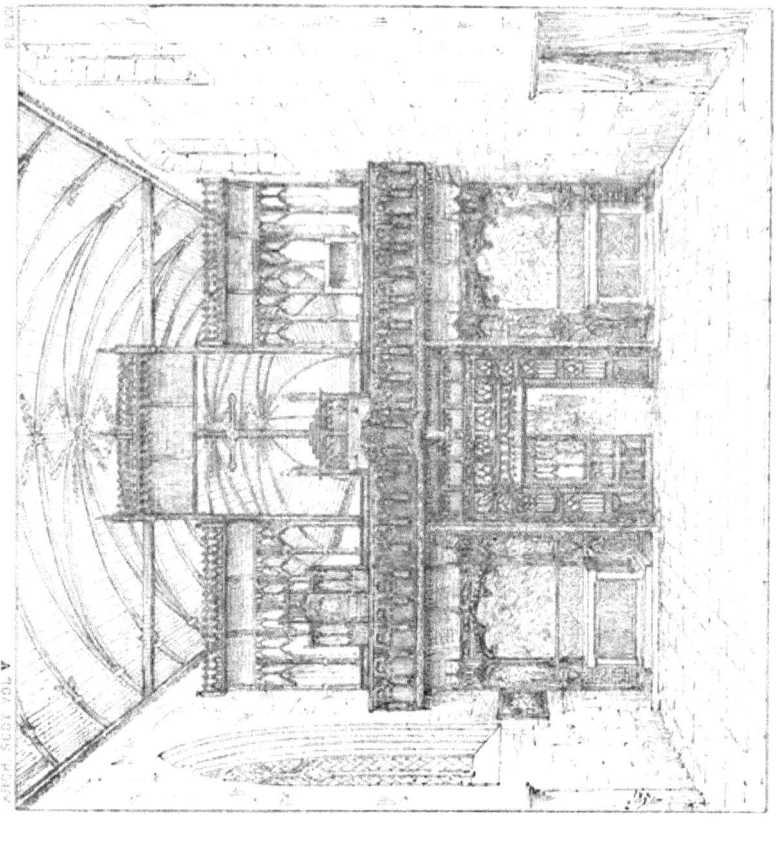

NAVE OF KING'S COLLEGE CHAPEL
SHOWING CONJECTURED ARRANGEMENT IN 1542

being occupied by the carved doorway communicating with the choir. Above this there remained till the other day a loft, with an ambone of carved oak over the doorway, while on either side extended a balustrade of the same pattern as the ambone. Of this only six panels are now seen and placed over the doorway, while the ambone and other six panels were carried away at the date of the last repairs of the chapel.

Tell-tale marks of nails in the niches of this gallery disclose that they were enriched with statues, and we know from the *Register* of 1542 that the subjects were the Saviour and the Apostles.[1]

Above this gallery there stretched across from wall to wall, near the roof, the three canopies which have been lowered and placed meaninglessly where the gallery was formerly.

These canopies are of rich design, and are perhaps unique in Britain. Up to the date when the chapel was last repaired (1872), they stood upon the oak framework, upon which they had been originally erected, covered with boarding on the west side to form the backs of bookcases, and separate the choir from the nave.

The central canopy is much the richest and deepest, and whether supported from below or not, it was attached to a beam which stretched across the church just above the top of the walls (and was possibly used as a Rood-beam before the canopies were made). The special importance given to the central canopy was no doubt due to its purpose, namely, to cover the great Crucifix, on either side of which were statues of the Virgin and of Saint John. Below these, on the gallery, was an altar—

"Altare solii crucifixi supra quod est crucifixus et statue dive Virginis et Joannis apostoli et evangeliste."

There was also on the loft the organ,[2] and on it a picture of the Virgin—

"In solio organorum. Organa ipsa cum imagine dive Virginis in superiore parte eorundem."

---

[1] The list of the furnishings of the chapel mentions not only "Velamen lineum pro usu quadragesimali cooperiens crucifixum et duas predictas statuas," but also "Velamen magnum ex lino, ante statuas Salvatoris et Apostolorum in facie solii crucifixi tempore quadragesimali appensum." *Fasti Aberd.*, p. 566, the spelling of Latin is given throughout, as the Register is printed in the *Fasti Aberdonenses*.

[2] The arrangement at Durham was, at one time, strikingly similar.

"There were three pairs of organs belonging to the said quire, for maintenance of God's service, and the better celebrating thereof. One of the fairest pair of the three stood over the quire door, only opened and played upon principal feasts." . . . . .

"Also there was a lantern of wood like unto a pulpit standing and adjoining to the wood-organs over the quire door, where they had wont to sing the nine lessons in the old time, on principal days, standing with their faces towards the high altar." (*Ancient Rites of Durham* (Davies). p. 27.)

I think it probable that the organ, in its case of **fine wainscot, with** the painting of the Virgin, stood under the north canopy, on the same side with the statue of the Virgin attached to the Holyrood.

We also find that on the loft was a picture **of the** Crucifixion. This is mentioned among the "parue tabule templi"—

"..... **Alia habens** imaginem crucifixi pendens supra solium organorum,"

and it may have been placed immediately beside the altar.

There were on the floor of the nave two altars, one to the Virgin to whom **the chapel was** dedicated, and whose name Bishop Elphinstone originally **intended the** College should bear—

"Altare **beate Marie Virginis** in nave ecclesie habens tabulam arte statuaria et duas statuas alteram ejusdem virginis, et alteram **beati** Kentigerni episcopi."[1]

The **other to** Saint German[2]—

"Altare sancti Germani habens tabulam arte statuaria et duas statuas alteram salvatoris flagellati alteram sancti Christophori."

These altars were almost certainly placed **one on** either side **of the door** entering into the choir. Altars in this position are still common **on the Continent.** When I first knew the Church of St Pierre at Louvain, the rood-screen (Plate LVIII. fig. 1) had altars in this position, **but they** have been removed. Still more remarkable as a *jubé* is the **beautiful** fantastic open gallery at Troyes (Plate LVIII. fig. 2). The choir screen of Glasgow shows altars **in** this position (Plate LVIII. **fig. 3**), and in the panels above them **there once were statues.**[3] At Exeter the lines of the arches (Plate LVIII. **fig. 4) on either side of the** door are admirably adapted to the style of the **carved oak at Aberdeen.**

---

[1] The saint of Glasgow, of which Bishop Elphinstone was a native, and at one time "Official," and Rector of the University, appears also on Elphinstone's seal (Laing's *Scottish Seals*, 1866, pl. x. fig. 8).

[2] Saint German had special claims on the attention of those who came to worship in the College chapel, for the revenues of his hospital in East Lothian had, by Royal charter, been diverted to the use of the College. There was some appropriateness in this diversion, for among what was given to the College we find the tithes of Glenmuick, Glengarden, and Slains, all in the adjoining district.

[3] While this paper was passing through the press, Archbishop Eyre, on 21st March, read a paper before the Archaeological Society of Glasgow, in which he says:—"On the left hand side of the Rood screen entrance was the altar of the Holy cross . . . . The altar of Our Lady, known as St Mary of Pity, stood at the right hand." The Archbishop assumed that the screen was erected by Bishop Blackader, on whose promotion Elphinstone was appointed Bishop of Aberdeen. This would make the two screens contemporary in date; but the President of the Society, Mr Honeyman, who has made a special study of the Cathedral, expressed a decided opinion that the Glasgow screen was older than the time of Blackader.

ROOD-SCREENS

In King's College Chapel we know that these spaces could not have been open, because the ancient stalls remain returning across the chapel, interrupted only by the open carved doorway.

One other feature I felt inclined to introduce into the conjectural sketch of the nave (Plate LVII.) as it must have originally appeared, namely, the desk of Bishop Elphinstone. Orem[1] speaks of it as "remaining entire" even in his day, and Pococke speaks of it a quarter of a century later. As preaching in the nave was contemplated by Elphinstone—the Principal and various other members of the College were each ordained "sexties in anno populo verbum Dei predicare"—it seems not unnatural that a seat should have been provided for his use.

I have only farther to remind those who would try to recall the impression and feeling of the nave as originally completed, not to forget "lights of discolored glass" spoken of by the translator of Boece—"the ancient bravery" of the parson of Rothiemay. All that could be said in 1772 was "some relics of their old splendour do yet remain."[2] The restoration of this feature was commenced with much taste in 1873 by the liberality of John Webster, Esq., LL.D., who has acquired public confidence in so remarkable a degree that, besides having been Lord Provost of and M.P. for Aberdeen, he has, ever since the passing of the Universities Act, been appointed by each successive Rector to the office of Lord Rector's Assessor.

The choir still used as the chapel is entered by the carved door in the choir screen. It is, indeed, robbed of much of the ancient glory of marble, and painting, and brass, and coloured hangings, and carpets on the pavement. But there remain the beautifully carved old oak stalls with their canopies and the *subsellia*, which will stand comparison with the best of those in the college chapels of Oxford and Cambridge. No one can but be struck with the appropriate simplicity, dignity, and solemnity of the building, and it is well that enough has survived to preserve the general tone and effect intended by the first architect.

All the stalls are there now as they were nearly four centuries ago, with perhaps no change, but the absence of a row of desks in front of the *subsellia*. Forty-two of the seats were appropriated to members of the College —the four doctors of theology (the Principal's),[3] canon law, civil law, and

---

[1] Page 173. *Fasti*, p. 58.   [2] Even in 1818 Kennedy says almost as much
[3] The Principal's being the first on the south on entering from the nave.

16 On the Chapel and Ancient Buildings of King's College, Aberdeen.

medicine, occupying the corner stalls. The curious on this subject may refer to Bishop Dunbar's charter. Most of the old carved *misereres* are gone, and all the back panels below the canopies, but not the framework of the panels. When I first remember the chapel, the oak was not varnished, and the framework of the panels was dark like the carved oak, but the panels were modern and light wainscot. They were stained dark at a comparatively recent date. I think I have been told that the original panels were carved with Gothic tracery, but were too much decayed to be repaired in 1823; and Douglas,[1] writing of the choir in 1780, says :—" On the west end, the stalls and back linings on the side walls are wainscot, and richly ornamented with most accurate carved work." If they were so carved, we may form a fair idea of the character of the ornament, from the back lining of the pulpit in the Collegiate Church of St Duthac at Tain (Plate LXII. fig. 1), said to have been presented by the Regent Murray. I have not discovered any authority but the *Statistical Account* of 1836 to support this tradition, but the Rev. William Taylor, who mentions it in his *Researches into the History of Tain*, was descended of a line of ancestors who had held the office of town clerk of Tain in unbroken succession from the time of Cromwell, so a more trustworthy tradition is not easily found. Had the tradition been that the pulpit was an offering from James IV., frequently a votary at the shrine of St Duthac, or from James V., who once, at least, worshipped there, or from Bishop Elphinstone, who was for a time Bishop of Ross, it would have been more natural. Murray is believed never to have been in Tain. Ross, the Provost of the Collegiate Church of St Duthac, must have met Murray at the Parliament of 1560, of which he was a member.

In the choir there was originally but one altar, but by the time of Bishop Stewart there were three.

1. The high altar in the apse. Upon it was a great picture—

"Una tabula magna arte pictoria miro ingenio confecta."

The Register of 1542 enables any one so minded to reconstruct Bishop Elphinstone's ideal of what was becoming for the service of the church.

We know exactly the appearance of the high altar of Notre Dame at Paris when Elphinstone studied there. Viollet le Duc assigns the four-

---

[2] *East Coast of Scotland*, p. 154.

CHAPEL KING'S COLLEGE
ABERDEEN UNIVERSITY

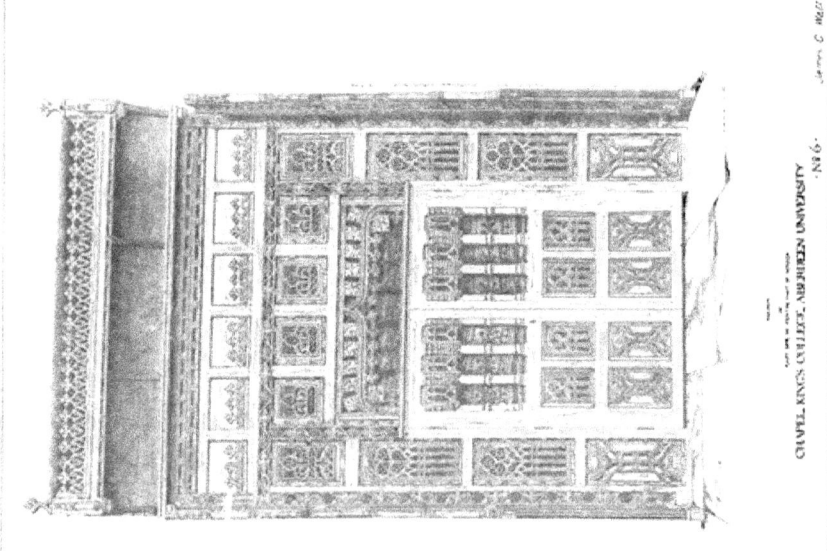

CHAPEL KING'S COLLEGE, ABERDEEN UNIVERSITY

teenth century as its date, and he gives, in his *Dictionnaire de L'Architecture*, voc. "Autel," from an engraving dated 1662, the drawing reproduced (Plate LXVII. fig. 3), with this description:—

"Quatre anges tenant les instruments de la passion sont posés sur quatre colonnes de cuivre portant les triangles sur lesquelles glissent les courtines. . . . . l'autel était fort simple, revêtu d'un parament, ainsi que le retable; derrière l'autel s'élevait le grand reliquaire contenant la chasse de Saint Marcel."

Having this description, when we read in the Aberdeen Register that there were among the furnishings in brass—

"Quatuor Columnæ, super quas effigies quatuor angelorum portantium insignia Christi;" "candelabrum enneum pendulum[1] coram summo altari;"

and also,

"Cortini templi," "perameuta"—

we can easily imagine what the high altar in King's College Chapel was like.

At Aberdeen the College was too near the Cathedral to possess relics of value likely to require a reliquary anything like so important as that at Paris, which would have run up to the ceiling. Still there was a

"Cistula miro artificio confecta et variis margaritis exornata pro reliquiis sanctorum et corporalibus,"

which may have been brought out on special occasions and placed over the great picture above referred to or on the retable behind the altar.

It is not easy to dispose of the sentences of the Register which follow that as to the quatuor columnæ—

"Sunt etiam super easdem columnas decem candelabra ennea.
Tria candelabra ennea pro luminibus in choro tempore hyemali.
Duo parva candelabra enea, ad ornatum altaris beatæ Catherine virginis."

I have been unable to have the MS. of the Register examined, and am inclined to suspect that the words *decem columnæ* may have been omitted or obliterated. But sometimes the curtains round the altars were supported by columns bearing angels carrying candles. An example is given, also from Viollet le Duc (Plate LVII. fig. 4); and the insignia of Christ may have been movable, and replaced by candelabra at certain festivals—as Candlemas.

2. The second altar of the choir was that "venerabilis sacramenti," probably on the north side as the place of honour. It and the "locus pro

---

[1] Well represented by another gift from Dr Webster.

sacramento figure pyramidalis,"[1] were both gifts of Alexander Galloway, a prebendary of the **Cathedral** and also Rector of the **University**. He gave also for this altar a statue "dive virginis patrone Collegii ex alabastro seu pario lapide," and a small picture "ex auro textili," and a brazen "lampas pendula" which hung in front of it.

3. The third altar was that "Beate Catherine Virginis," adorned with "Tabula continens effigies nostri domini et divarum Catharine et Barbare." This altar was also a votive erected by the executors of Hector Boece, the **first Principal**. It was most likely on the south side of the choir.

The removal of the oak panelling **at this end** of the chapel would almost certainly disclose, by markings on the wall, where these altars were fixed, and whether they were placed along the wall or at right angles to it; also at what point the steps up to the high altar occurred, and how many steps there were. There are two corbels, one on either side just westward of the apse. These may have been used in fixing up—

"Velum magnum ex candenti lino infra chorum et magnum altare tempore quadragesimali appensum,"—

if so, they would show the length of the platform of the high altar. But the first rise must have commenced farther west, for **Orem** (*Registrum*, p. 174) says that the tomb of Elphinstone was on the first step of the altar. In that case the second step would be to the east of the tomb, and after a like space probably three more steps close to each other led to the platform.

Besides these altars the **chief** features of the choir must have been the hanging lamps, and candelabra of brass, of which there were about a score, and the three **brazen ambones**, at which the Gospel, the Epistle, **and** the Legenda were read.

"Unus pro evangelio cantando; alter pro epistola et tertius pro legenda,"

—something more than "lecterns," in the modern sense, I presume, as they are, by Boece in his Life of Elphinstone, alluded to as "cathedræ."

The two first, no doubt, were on the same platform as the high altar. In foreign churches *sedilia*, such as we are familiar with in England for

---

[1] *Fasti*, p. 565. **Very likely** this "locus pyramidalis" may have been as high as the stalls; **but if** it had run up to the roof, similar examples could easily be quoted. It would still have been described as pyramidal. There is not a single piece of carving but this in the whole chapel which could be described as pyramidal.

CHOIR OF KINGS COLLEGE CHAPEL BEFORE THE REFORMATION

the officiating clergy, were not common. I cannot say what the general rule was in Scotland, but stone *sedilia* were not uncommon. Abroad brazen chairs were frequently used, sometimes highly ornate. More commonly, they and the lecterns were made very simply of metal rods. The ambone for the "legenda" must have stood between the stalls.

The whole would derive colour from the "much pretious stuffe layde up" in the shape of tapestry and carpets, for the altars and walls and pavement in front of the high altar and for the choir. The Register shows how much of this was "attrabaceum" from Arras, then the great emporium of such work.

The last and not the least prominent feature must have been the tomb of Bishop Elphinstone, and we have the detailed description of it in the inventory of 1542, which tells us that the statue of the bishop lay, as was most natural, arrayed in his pontificals, on the upper stone, which was supported by statues of the three Theological Virtues and Contemplation on the south, and the Cardinal Virtues on the north :—

"Sepulchrum domini Fundatoris, in cujus superiore parte imago ipsius in pontificalibus, cum duobus angelis portantibus duo candelabra ad caput, et duobus mercenariis epitaphium in ore insculptum ad pedes portantibus: inferius, ex australi parte, tres virtutes theologice et Contemplatio, in boreali virtutes cardinales suis signis distinctæ; in orientali et occidentali partibus domini Fundatoris insignia ab angelis lata."[1]

From these details it would be easy to restore the tomb. The spirit of restoration of ancient monuments is spreading so fast that it is not unreasonable to hope that the tomb may once more be made worthy of one of the best bishops Scotland ever saw.

The next notice we have of it is in 1661 from Gordon of Rothiemay.

"In this church William Elphingstoune lyes buryed, his tombe-stone of black towtch-stone; the upper pairt upheld of old by thretteine statues of brasse; his statue of brasse lying betwixt the two stons"; "all these robbed and sold long agoe."[2]

The only other allusions to the tomb I have observed are those of J. Macky[3]—"Here is a fine monument of Bishop Elphinstone;" and Orem,[4] who speaks of this tomb as "*lately* stripped of its canopy and ornaments, for fear of accidents, and reduced to a plain blue marble slab." It is

---

[1] *Fasti*, p. 563.   [2] *Description of the Two Towns of Aberdeen.*
[3] *Journey through Scotland*, p. 41, published in 1723.
[4] Or a narrative usually incorporated with his work, but dated 1771, p. 41.

strange that so remarkable a feature as a canopy remained unnoticed if it existed. The date of the destruction of Elphinstone's tomb nowhere appears. Principal Anderson got credit for saving the chapel from the mob in 1580, and it is not mentioned in the official reports 1618-28[1] as to dilapidation of the buildings, during the time of Bishop Patrick Forbes, who died in 1638. Gordon mentions no particulars in his history, which contains so detailed an account of the mischief done in Old Aberdeen by the Covenanting party during and after the meeting of the General Assembly in Aberdeen in 1640.

It is not easy to estimate the effect upon the art of a district—of workmen being familiar with examples of high taste—and I cannot but think that the tomb of Elphinstone educated the Aberdeen carpenter, who on 14th December 1636 "was ordainit" by the magistrates "to big and erect in most decent and comelie forme, ane loft within the yle of the Grayfrier kirk of this burghe, befoir the pulpett, for the use of proucst, baillies, and counsall."

How he performed his task, and how the result was regarded when the General Assembly met at Aberdeen in 1640, we learn from Gordon:[2]— "That yeare or not long befor the magistratts of Aberdeen had tackne panes for to repaire the Grayfreer Church, and had adorned it with a costly seate, in a lofte just opposite to the pulpitt. The carpenter had showed his skill in cutting upon the several compartments of the frontispeece of that lofte the figures of Faith, Hope, and Charity, and the Moral Vertwes, as they use to be painted emblem wyse: There stood Faithe leaning upon the Cross. This was as soon quarrelled at as espyed by severall ministers, commissioners of the Assemblye, who looked upon all that new frontispeece as savouring of superstitione, and wold needs have Faithe or her Crosse removed from ther. The magistratts durst not excuse it; and many others were silent least they should be suspected. In ende Mr Andrew Ramsay, the moderator, interposed himself, ... so that by his mediatione they were pacifyd, and Faith with the rest of the Vertwes were permitted to stand still, wheir they as yett remain undefaced to this daye."

Bishop Forbes, "the best prelate," says Spottiswood, "that Scotland had seen since Elphinstone," seems to have re-established public preaching in the nave, and to have used the choir, among other purposes, for meetings of

---

[1] *Fasti Aberd.*, p. 6.   [2] *Scots Affairs*, vol. iii. p. 219.

INTERIOR OF CHOIR, KINGS COLLEGE CHAPEL FROM EAST 1542

the Synod of his diocese.[1] Here he set up his own throne, or rather seat, where the altar was, above the steps leading up to the apse, and arranged pews rising on either side from Elphinstone's tomb to the windows, painting on each pew the name of the presbytery whose members were to occupy it. All these remained till 1823, including his seat. The canopied back of it is there still, with a modern oak pulpit placed in front of it in 1828, when Sunday services within the walls of the university were resumed. The desk or front of his seat was at that time removed to the north side of the chapel, and used for the seat occupied by the professor acting as "hebdomadarius." It is now used as a base for Bishop Stewart's pulpit. My father gave me the history of this piece of oak, and no one can look at it, and at the back of the pulpit in the apse, without admitting that they belong to each other.

Bishop Forbes is said to have erected a second throne or seat, in the nave on the right side of the carved door, while he placed a pulpit on the other side for the public preaching above referred to. They could only have been placed in that position after the altars of the Virgin and Saint German were removed. This is not a matter of oral tradition; I have read it somewhere recently, but, unfortunately, cannot give the reference.[2] Note 3 reconciles what I had written with what Orem says (p. 173), referring to the choir of the church, "There is a hearse in it," probably one of the original candelabra referred to in the inventory of 1542, "and the bishop's seat or pulpit in the east end thereof, where the altar stood formerly, with presbytery's desks on every side thereof;" "in this chapel there is a middle wall of timber and above it an excellent loft, with a pulpit on the left side thereof, where the priest preached, and Bishop Elphinstone's desk below the said loft yet remains entire, in it likewise is the organ loft entire." Thus, besides the "gallery with a pulpit or ambon there were two pulpits or desks, one on each side of the door. Till after the time of Bishop Forbes, the organ as well as the loft had remained entire; "in the University of Old Aberdeen there stood the remainder of ane old organ, upon which was painted, in a course draught, the pourtraicte of some woman, nobody

---

[1] And here for 200 years the Synods of Aberdeen, whether Episcopalian or Presbyterian, continued to meet.

[2] I presume a bishop has no throne except in the cathedral of his diocese.

[3] Since this sentence was penned, I have seen Bishop Pococke's *Tour in Scotland*, 1760, p. 207. He writes of King's College Chapel:—"The church is an oblong square, and the body is divided from the Quire by a fine Covered Screen and Gallery, with a pulpit in it, and under that are two Carved Seats. . . . The Stalls of the Quire are of the same beautifull Gothic carved work."

could tell who, and had hunge there half brokne, wholly neglected for many years; this was brokne downe and complained upon," when the General Assembly met at Aberdeen in 1640, "as a thing very intollerable in the churche of a College;"[1] and again, "Anno 1642, Principal Guild[2] causit tak doune the organ case qubilk wes of fyne wanescot and had stand within the kirk since the Reformation."

Notwithstanding all the changes that took place, the pipes of the organ were still lying on the organ loft in the present century, as I have been told by those who had seen them there.

We do not hear of preaching in the nave after the Reformation, except in 1642 by Principal Guild, who seems to have got small thanks for his trouble, and in 1720 by Principal Chalmers, who seems to have met with as little support. Bishop Pococke tells us, in 1760, "this Church is not used but for giving degrees," and the students marched on Sundays to the Cathedral-Machar's kirk, where they occupied "the College loft," at least from 1634 to 1823.

A great change, however, came over the nave in its conversion into the University library. The original library, as has been mentioned, was built on the south side of the chapel, over class-rooms and beside the chapter house and "jewell house." Like the rest of the building, it had by 1618 fallen into great disrepair, and the whole roof was ordered to be taken off, and put in order and covered with lead. We see it in

---

[1] Gordon, *Scots Affairs* (ed. Spald.), vol. iii. p. 218.

[2] Dr Guild, or Goold as he is often called, was one of those who at first stoutly objected to Presbytery, and gave up his professorship at Aberdeen, and retired to Holland, rather than sign the Covenant; but he afterwards returned, and getting a church in Aberdeen, signed it with qualifications, and on the bait of the Principalship of King's College being offered, he swallowed it entire, and showed his zeal by many unfortunate acts of destroying ancient ecclesiastical buildings. This naturally roused the Prelatists, who speak of him always with a sneer. Bishop Forbes's revival of preaching in the nave was highly approved by them, but when some years after his death Dr Guild tried to have them resumed, here is the way his efforts are recorded :—"Wednesday, 6 April 1642, Dr Goold began to preiche within the College kirk ane weiklie sermon to be taught that day to the old toun people, studentis, maisteris and memberis of the College. This ordour seemit strange, to preiche outwith Maucher Kirk, as was sumtymis usit befoir, and bring down the people, man, wyf and maidis to the College kirk, among young scolleris and studentis . . . . . The gryt bellis of the College and Maucher kirk rang both thric tymes to ilk sermon, for conveining ane auditoris, quhilk wes never usit befoir, and whiche schortlie decayit to his disgrace, as he justlie deservit." Again, "Upone Wednesday, 4 May, Doctor Goold, principall, began a noveltie, and to preiche upone this welk day within the College Kirk at Old Aberdene. . . . . His auditoures war feu, who had littell feist of the doctrein, and at last himself wyreit, and shortlie gave over this weiklie sermon moir foolishlie nor it began."—Spalding, *State Affairs*, vol. ii. p. 141. He had more serious troubles in store, for he was deprived of the Principalship by Monk's four generals, who were sent to reform the University.

PULPIT OF ST DUTHAC, TAIN

1540
BISHOP STEWART'S PULPIT

BISHOP PATRICK FORBES DESK

Gordon's sketch (Plate **LV.** fig. 2), in its restored state, nearly flat, and leaning against the chapel wall. A century later, on 3rd September 1719, we find the masters of the College " took a view of the library in order to make some reparations for accommodating severall books that are lying loose," and ordered some temporary work to serve " untill such time as the College shall be **in a condition to** enlarge the said library, by taking down the partition wall **on the east end**"—there being by this time, unfortunately, no longer occasion for the " jewell house." Happily, the state of the library was brought specially to the notice of an old alumnus, Dr Fraser, physician to the King and treasurer of Chelsea Hospital.[1] Through his generosity, the old building was taken down, and new class-rooms erected **on the** ground floor, and a new library above nearly double the length **of** the old **one.** This room must have been about 70 feet long. There is reason to suppose that the roof was no longer flat, but raised in the centre.

"Bibliotheca nova longitudine duplo fere aucta ac quatuor scholæ infra positæ Græcarum literarum et Philosophiæ prælectionibus sacratæ, ab imis fundamentis polito lapide pulcherrimum in modum extruuntur."[1]

The same authority **tells of the effect of the rebuilding, which he** mainly effected, of **the** south side of the quadrangle erected by Bishop Dunbar—

"Area sublimibus fulget decorata columnis,
Marmore de Parco; cuncta superba micant."[2]

When next the library is heard of, it occupied the nave of the chapel ; Dr Fraser's library (completed in 1725) and the class-rooms below had been destroyed by fire.

I first heard of this from my father, in reply to my asking how the **north** side of the chapel came to **be** of fresh-looking granite, while there were embedded in it a number of coats of arms evidently of much more ancient date, and carved in sandstone. He told me there had been a library there, which had been burnt, and that when this happened the chapel wall required **new** support, and **was** then cased and buttressed with granite as **we now see** it ; **and** that the old coats of arms had been nearly all on the **walls of the** library, and having escaped the fire, were along with some others inserted in the new granite work.

I have heard my mother tell of this burning. She had the story

---

[1] " Vir nunquam sine laude nominandus," as says the inscription on the chapel wall, although not one stone of his work has been allowed to remain upon another.   [2] *Fraserades*, pp. 11 and 20.

from her father, Principal Macleod, and said that it took place during his connection with the university. I do not recollect any date being mentioned. The professor, who was "hebdomadar" for the week, and so in charge of the buildings, had one afternoon, after the students' dinner at which he had, *ex officio*, presided, put his hand on some wainscotting, and finding it very hot, suspected fire, and caused some of the lining of the room where he was to be torn down, when fire burst out, and there was barely time to save the books of the library by "throwing them into the nave of the chapel," then "neglected and disused," and there they remained till 1870, when the present new library was built.

Dr Fraser's library, like its predecessor, was not on the ground floor, as we have just seen. I venture to suggest that the books may have been, in part at least, thrown into the nave of the chapel by the door which communicated with the organ loft, the existence of which was ascertained when the book presses were removed. So far as I know, that door was the only access to that gallery.[1] No doubt the principal access to the library was from the quadrangle,—perhaps from the porch at the south door; but following the analogy of other such buildings, there probably was an access from the chapter-house, as at Crossraguel—or the "jewell house"—to the library, and this would form the most convenient communication for those officiating in the choir to pass to the gallery, unless there was either a narrow wooden stair behind one of the altars in the nave, or a stair in the thickness of the wall. Unfortunately, when the library shelving and even

---

[1] I believe no trace of a wooden stair to the rood loft was discovered. The late Mr Matheson, then of H.M. Office of Works, promised me that I should be informed before the replastering of the walls commenced, but I was not warned in time to reach Aberdeen until after the walls had been all lathed, and had their first coat of plaster. Those in charge, however, were most obliging, and offered to remove the lath at any point I chose. I did not trust my own skill in such matters sufficiently to feel warranted in acting largely on this offer, but I could not resist the opportunity of testing an opinion I had long entertained that the organ loft had been approached by a door on its level on the south wall, and the plaster, when broken, accordingly disclosed the door, which has since been left uncovered, to tell the position of the gallery. This door, and the mark on the roof where the beam above the canopies was fixed, determine exactly the original position of the old carved oak work. The door is small certainly, 4 feet × 2—but many a smaller door of access to rood lofts is to be found in old churches—and it was filled up with bricks, and therefore it was said it must be modern. Those who stated this view probably did not know that there had been a library immediately outside, in which the books required for use in the gallery may have been kept. But before the library was burned—the organ was silent, and the voice of the preacher was dumb in the nave—a door in that position could no longer be of use, and might have been built up when Fraser's enlargement of the library took place, and if still open must necessarily have been built up, when after the fire the wall was cased in granite from the ground to the foot of the chapel windows.

NAVE OF KINGS COLLEGE CHAPEL, FITTED UP AS LIBRARY.
1770.

the stalls were removed from the wall in 1873, I understand that no one made a thorough examination of the walls, from an ecclesiological point of view, to see how far there were traces of old stairs or doors.

It is not easy to fix precisely the date of the destruction of the library built by Dr Fraser. We know from Bishop Pococke that in 1760 the nave was not fitted up for a library; and in 1769 Pennant speaks of the chapel as "ruinous within," with no hint that it was occupied by the library, of which he speaks at some length, but on April 7, 1772, a resolution was adopted by the Senatus to fit up the nave as a library, and to use the materials of the library and schools in erecting the new professors' houses. That library and the lecture rooms had been the pride of the University, and were not fifty years old. Some catastrophe must have led to their destruction. The nave might have been used as an enlargement of the library to meet the increasing accumulation of books under the Copyright Act of Queen Anne, without destroying that built by Dr Fraser. Moreover, the public school, where the students in 1760 met for prayers (see next page), came to be divided into class-rooms, which could only have been required by the destruction of those under Fraser's library. Douglas, who gives the first description of the library when occupying the nave of the chapel, wrote as in 1780, and makes not the slightest allusion to Dr Fraser's building, but does allude to the existence of the two, then new, detached professors' houses at the south-west corner of the College, which are evidently built with granite from the same quarry as the casing of the chapel. Matters did not move fast in those days, but we may infer that not much time was allowed to elapse between the fire and the fitting up of classrooms for the students, and providing accommodation for the library. The six pages of a notice of Old Aberdeen, bearing date 1771, and printed with Orem's work, pp. 39-45, describes Fraser's library as still existing. The date—1772 or 1773—would tally equally with the tradition that the fire took place in my grandfather's time, and with the story of the conflict with the sailors when the new houses were being built.

The next stage of interest in the history of the chapel we do not reach till 1823. From the time of Bishop Patrick Forbes, the choir had been used for the meetings of the Synod of Aberdeen, for which he had fitted it up, and for competitions for the chair of theology, the only chair in Scotland filled up by public competition. The founder of the chair made members of the Presbyteries of the Synod and three Professors the judges, and appointed the competition to take place here, as it has done ever since. It was used also for various academic functions, such as graduation ceremonies. Here, too, the students met for morning prayers after the fire,[1]—not at the date of Bishop Pococke's visit, for he says,—"This church is not used except for giving degrees. In the room where they have morning and evening prayer is a large desk hung with a fine carpet, in which the King's and Bishop Elphinstone's arms are worked"—beyond doubt one of the aulea magna on which the Register more than 200 years before recorded that "Regia insignia simul atque fundatoris sunt intexta." Where is such carpet-work to be found now? I remember seeing the table—a long old-fashioned many-legged one—of the room where the Senatus used to meet covered with a carpet; and the front of "the College loft" in St Machar's, till it was removed about 1860, was also hung with carpets. Were these also some of Elphinstone's furnishing?

How early the choir ceased to be used for ordinary Sunday services does not appear, but in 1634 the Principal was censured for remissness in "going to the kirk before the studentis," and there is early mention of "the College loft" in the cathedral. Down to 1823 the students of the Arts classes, after meeting and receiving instruction from their various professors, marched to the cathedral in their scarlet gowns up the narrow street, in which most of the houses stood gablewise to the roadway, with space between them for eaves-drop from the heavy thatched roofs.

I have heard old students amusing each other by confessing the shortcomings of their college days, and among others, that of having, when they thought they were unobserved, slipped up one or other of these eaves-drop slits, and let the procession pass on; but they had also to tell of being occasionally detected, and dragged out in disgrace.

It was not improbably the recollection of such scenes that prompted Dr Alexander Murray of Philadelphia, a graduate of the University, in making his will in 1793, to bequeath part of his estate, subject to the liferent of his widow—

---

[1] John Thomson, "the sacrist," the "singular" if not apostolic successor of the chaplain mentioned in the charter as having charge of the fabric and furnishings of the church, and his associate David Cromar—"John and Davie," as they were called—used, with a mixture of shame and pride, to point out names of professors who, while students, had been so irreverent as to carve them on the oak.

KING'S COLLEGE, OLD ABERDEEN.

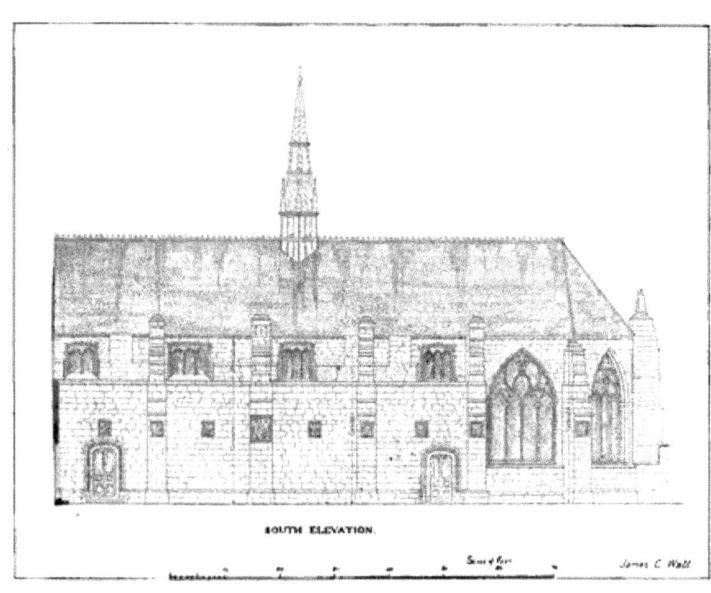

SOUTH ELEVATION.

James C. Watt

"For the encouragement, in the first place, of a clergyman to preach a course of lectures in their College church on Sunday mornings . . . This donation **is also intended to** remove in some measure the uncommon grievance and indecorum of their processions to their Parish Church, in an inclement and dangerous season. In this unprejudiced critical age it were to be wished **that** this famous seminary would agree upon a form of public prayer and worship with or without responses, and instrumental **musie,** to be read at these lectures, as is common in all other countries, to **move the youth** to the greater solemnity and order."

On this bequest becoming available through Mrs Murray's **death, about** the time when the west front of the College was being rebuilt, chiefly **by means of** a public subscription, the restoration of the choir and its re-adaptation as a College chapel was at once undertaken.

Up to that time the steps to the high altar had remained untouched, and then Bishop Forbes's throne was bisected and used, as already told.[1] Behind the desk in its new position was placed an oak panel with Bishop Elphinstone's arms, at that time removed from the old hall (Plate LXX.).

A deeply carved door may be noticed at the east **end of** the stalls, **on the south side of** the chapel, where no door is usually found. This **door was** removed from the cathedral (Plate LXVII.) **when** it was being re-pewed early in the present century, and it owes its place in the College chapel to the fact that a carpenter employed in the cathedral was also **engaged** in repairing the chapel. Many of the old pews in the cathedral had been made to the fancy of the occupiers, and the carpenter had so admired this door that he saved it when the rest of the old work was swept away, and was glad when he secured it a position where it could be both preserved and admired.[2] There was also used,—first as "the censor's" desk, and

---

[1] *Supra,* p. 433.
[2] He was a worthy successor of the carpenter who refused to take part in the destruction of the reredos of the altar of the cathedral till the evil work was commenced by the parish minister, Mr John Strachan, at the instigation, it is said, of Dr Guild. Strachan was a remarkable man, and by what inconsistency or crotchetiness of character he was led to such an act it is difficult to imagine. Here is Orem's account of him condensed :—He was a professor as well as parish minister. He was the best scholar that ever was in the college. He was to graduate his scholars, and after he had printed his theses, and distributed them, and the day appointed for the graduation in the common school of the college, Mr Andrew Cant, regent in Marischall College, and others, said he had set down Popish portions in his thesis. But Mr Strachan told them he would defend all that was inserted in his theses ; whereupon the place of graduation was altered from the College to St Machar's Church. When the day **came,** there was a great confluence of gentry; then came over the Cants, and all the rest of the clergy of

subsequently used as the "precentor's,"—another piece of carved wood. It also came from the cathedral, and is somewhat in the style of Bishop Stewart's pulpit, but probably later.

Whether the east window had ever been opened, in obedience to the order of 1619, repeated in 1638, I do not know,[1] but it was in 1823 dealt with as we now see it, the monument to the younger Seougal being moved and inserted above the pulpit. This monument Orem tells us was on the north side of the chapel. "He lies interred in the College chapel on the north side thereof, opposite to the high altar now called the Bishop's seat or desk; with an inscription upon the wall above his grave . . . . . 'Multa in tam brevissimo curriculo didicit, præstitit, docuit. Cœli avidus et cœlo maturus, obiit anno dom. MD.CLXXVIII. Ætatis suæ xxviii.'"[2]

One other notable change was made in the appearance of the chapel in 1823, viz., the hanging on the walls of five large paintings of Scripture subjects. They used to hang outside of the old hall in the vestibule, which was long used as the Senatus room. The round ivy tower which abuts on it, the spire of which was blown down on Candlemas Day 1715,[3] and never restored;[4] and the tower and three-light window of the vestibule, were the chief features of the south side of the college till the new class-rooms were built.

The paintings may probably enough be of the date of Jameson, and painted by his scholars. The subjects were, The Meeting of Jephtha and his Daughter, David slaying Goliath, The Judgment of Solomon, The Queen of Sheba, David and Abigail. The only one I have any recollection of

---

Aberdeen, and placed themselves in the Marquess of Huntley's loft, opposite to the pulpit; for Mr Strachan had taken the pulpit. Mr Strachan began with a prayer, and after he had a long harangue, he invited them to impugn his theses. Then they began to object, and he answered their arguments readily; but they all answered uno ore, which made a great confusion. When this dispute was ended, coming out of the church door, Mr Strachan accuses young Mr Andrew Cant for some reflecting answer in the dispute, and would have trampled him under his feet, if the gentry had not interposed. "For Mr Strachan was a gentleman, and a pretty man, both in parts and in body, and undervalued all the Cants." He afterwards resigned his chair, turned Popish, and died at the head of the Scots College at Paris. Notwithstanding his victory, however, I suspect the name of Cant is more familiar within the walls of the university than that of Strachan.

[1] One window was closed up anno 1715 (Orem, p. 173). It was reopened by an order of the Senatus in 1821.   [2] Orem, p. 191.   [3] Orem, p. 182.

[4] It was mainly owing to the efforts of Dr John Hill Burton, the historian, that this tower was preserved; and now that the hall and its window have been removed and replaced by a much loftier building, the tower, which is still interesting as a landmark, would require the replacing of the quaint old spire to give it effect and significance.

University Buildings Old Aberdeen
from
South West 1889.

King's College from South West 1850.

having seen elsewhere treated identically was the Judgment of Solomon, which I once saw painted on copper on a very small scale.

These pictures were removed from the vestibule, or "lobby," as it was then called, of the hall, with no intention of their being replaced anywhere. But the sacrist and janitor "John and Davie" had always admired them, and wishing to contribute to the adornment of the chapel, carefully preserved them, had them varnished by the village painter, and, after all the repairs had been completed and the day was fixed for their official inspection, they had them during the night erected on the chapel walls over the stalls and over the west door.

Regard for two faithful servitors, I believe, rather than the desire to preserve specimens of early Scottish paintings, led to their being left on the walls, to the astonishment of many an English tourist, who could hardly believe their eyes when they thought they saw ante-Reformation pictures allowed to remain on Presbyterian walls. I believe they are now elsewhere preserved for their value in the history of Scottish art.[1]

Only one other change was made in the chapel, so far as I can recollect, before the recent remodelling of it. The Senatus got from the kirk-session of Old Machar the remains of a pulpit which had been erected in the cathedral by Bishop Stewart, the builder of the original College library. Orem, when telling of the destruction wrought by the fall of the great central steeple of the cathedral on 9th May 1688, remarks (p. 109):—"The pulpit built by the said Bishop Stewart, as witness his name on it, was also preserved, being removed some time before the fall of said steeple." It had the "arms of Christ" carved on it; but a party of Covenanters

---

[1] To the question put to me by one of the Professors, How would it do to hang them now in the nave? the reply might be given, it would secure their preservation, and being seen better than any other position that they are likely to be placed in, and it would be putting the nave to a better use than the nave of the greater King's College chapel at Cambridge was put on the occasion of Queen Elizabeth's visit. It appears (Mr T. J. Proctor Carter's *King's College Chapel, Cambridge*, pp. 59 and 60) that the authorities not only prepared a place for her Majesty in the quire—"Also a fair closet glazed towards the quire was devised and made in the middle of the rood-loft; if the Queen's Majestie would perhaps there repose herself; which was not occupied. At the same time a theatre had been erected in the anti-chapel against the rood loft, the chantries on either side serving as green-rooms for this somewhat inappropriately placed stage. Here on the following day the scholars of the college performed with great success the Aulularia of Plautus for the diversion of the queen and her court." Speak of Presbyterian want of reverence for churches after this! James V., in 1541, and his Queen visited Aberdeen, and had their quarters in the College, and were entertained with "divers triumphes and playes and comedies," but we have no hint that they were performed in the chapel.

(The Master of Forbes . . . . . Dr Guild, Principal, *pro pudor!*), on 5th August 1640, "came all ryding up the gate, came to Machar Kirk, and ordained our blessed Lord Jesus Christ his armes to be hewn out of the foir front of the pulpit thereof." It seems to have been used as the ordinary pulpit of the cathedral till the reseating early in the century already referred to, when it was cast aside as lumber into a room at the bottom of the north-west steeple, its place being taken by a very well-designed mahogany one with Corinthian pillars.[1] After some thirty or forty years, it was given to the University on condition of its re-erection. Its whole framework was complete, and one or two panels which were in part wanting were restored from the fragments that remained. The canopy seems the most doubtful part of it, but I remember well that the carpenter employed was quite confident that what remained of the old work demonstrated the accuracy of the restoration he was ordered to carry out. Besides its being an interesting memorial of one of the greatest benefactors of the College, and a good specimen of oak carving of its date, it is amusing to think of it as the pulpit from which Strachan defied the Cants. It will be observed that it was originally designed to be fixed against one of the round pillars of the cathedral. Unfortunately, no part of the base remained, and the desk of Bishop Forbes's seat was used, being nearly a century later in style and quite incongruous. It is high time that it should be replaced where Forbes placed it, in the east end of the chapel and in front of his canopy. Its position there would be in point of fact historically accurate,—certainly consistent with early ecclesiastical usage as to the position of a Bishop's seat,—and not unimportant as an index of the feelings of one of the most respected of the bishops of the Reformed Episcopal Church, notwithstanding the suggestion of the editor of the *Fasti Aberdonenses*, that the good bishop would have been displeased to see it where it is.[2]

We have now traced the chapel down to the present date. It was, I believe, mainly due to the efforts of the Chancellor, the Duke of Richmond, and of the Principal, Dr Peter Campbell, who interested himself in every-

---

[1] Surely St Machar's Church has been singularly unfortunate in the taste of those who have superintended its repairs from time to time. No greater mistake could have been made in such a building than substituting the mahogany pulpit for a 200 years old oak one, unless it was removing the mahogany one, excellent of its kind, for as mean a structure in the way of pulpit as ever disfigured the most unpretentious of parish churches.

[2] *Fasti*, p. lvii.

thing that concerned the University as much as if **he had** been an alumnus —Edinburgh was his *alma mater*—that the chapel, the roof of which was found to be in a dangerous state of decay, was taken charge of and restored by H.M. Office of Works.

I have seen the opinion stated **more than once**, that the roof and spire of the chapel are evidently of the middle of the 17th century.[1] I am aware of no warrant for this opinion except the occurrence of the name of Charles II. on the lead.[2] This can do no more than suggest that it was repaired in his reign. If, as seems probable, not only the design of the chapel but **the woodwork itself** be foreign, it is unsafe to try and fix dates by changes of style in this country. The earliest notice I have observed of the spire is under date "15 June 1638," when a report was obtained from the "Dean of gild of Aberdeine," associated with "a wright" and "a plumbear," "who gaue ther judgement in maner following:—Imprimis, they found ruiff of the kirk, for ought they can persaue, sufficient, except it be in sylling **and sarking**. Secundo, they find it neidful that the south syde of the kirke be tirrit . . . . . from the litle steipill to the east gavill of the kirk; and the litle stipill itself bothe theikit with leid and repairit in the timber wark." If it was old enough in 1638 to require repairs, we may be very certain that it dates from the 16th century; and, looking to the history of the times, it is probably coeval with the chapel, the contract for covering which with lead is dated in 1506.[4]

Gratitude to those who procured the repair of the chapel in 1873 must be tempered by regret for some of the things that were done, or rather that were left undone.

A **new library was built**, which left the nave available **for securing** more space for the enlarged wants of the University after the union of King's and Marischal Colleges, and so the stalls were moved westwards one bay, after having been faithfully gone over and repaired. The change was **a reasonable one, but it alters** considerably the original proportions. The **shortening of the nave by** one-third **cramps** it and takes **from its dignity,** while adding to the choir **seems to lower the roof.** But much more serious mischief was done than this, **for alas!** in carrying out this scheme, the old

---

[1] *Fasti Aberd.*, p. lix.
[2] The lead of the chapel roof was authorised to be sold, and slates substituted, in 1793
[3] *Fasti Aberd.*, p. 410.   [4] *Ibid.*, p. lvii.

historical organ gallery with its ambone was ruthlessly destroyed. The Reformers had not seen occasion to destroy it; they had been satisfied with the removal, probably by the hands of the members of the University, of all the carved figures great and small, and of the paintings of the Virgin and of the Crucifixion. They left the organ in its place, and when the nave was turned into the library, the Senatus had the taste to preserve the beautiful gallery and its ambone and the three canopies, although plans which involved their destruction were laid before them by an architect.

We have already (page 434) quoted Pococke's reference to the screen in 1760; it is thus noticed by Douglas in 1780:—

"Above the books, on the east end, is some very curious carved work on the boards which divide the library from the chapel, to humour which, the cross gallery has ancient rails; but in my opinion they neither look well nor at all correspond with the modern ones," an opinion which few will concur in who turn to Billing's drawing of the library.[1]

The screen, however, was not removed till its beauty and historical value had been recognised by many ecclesiologists.

From this point of view Dean Stanley has pointed out its great interest, and has selected it as the typical one in Britain. "Nothing," he says, "can be more splendid than the ambones in the church at Ravillo, near Amalfi, which, though long deserted, remain a witness to the predominant importance attributed in ancient times to the reading of the Bible in the public services. In the French Church the very name of the lofty screens which parted the nave from the choir bears testimony to the same principle. They were called *Jube* from the opening words of the introduction of the gospel *Jube Domine*. Those that still exist, like that of Troyes, and also in the King's College at Aberdeen, by their stately height and broad platforms, show how imposing must have been this part of the service, now so humiliated and neglected. Few such now remain."[2]

It is melancholy to think that to the list of jubès which have perished, must now, at least for the present, be added that of King's College. That the altars, statues, and statuettes should have disappeared at the time of the Reformation was only natural; but that the gallery and ambone should have been thrown aside in 1873, would have seemed to me almost incredible

---

[1] *Baronial and Ecclesiastical Remains*, vol. 1.
[2] Stanley's *Christian Institutes*, p. 55.

ROODSCREEN, CROSCOMBE CHURCH, NEAR WELLS.
(*Reproduced from the Magazine of Art by permission of the Publishers.*)

were the fact not one within my own knowledge and that of hundreds; and why should those three canopies have been lowered to a new and utterly meaningless position, however effective [1] from their intrinsic beauty, and this after they had remained where originally placed for two hundred years after the latest burst of fanaticism which discredited the Reformation?

Was it in compliance with the order of the architect, or in bitter irony, that the carpenter who lowered the canopy nailed to it the hideous grotesque which till lately deformed the chapel?

Glasgow alone, I believe, in Scotland has the distinction of having retained its stone choir screen. In Linlithgow, the screen survived to the present century. At Lincluden there are very interesting remains of a stone one, with niches and statuettes. At Fowlis Easter there are some fragments of a wooden one and of paintings connected with it. It would be endless to discuss in detail all the traces of them still to be found in Scotland.[2]

Can anything now be done to repair the mischief of 16 years ago?

To restore so much of the old gallery and screen and canopies as would not offend the most sensitive Protestant, and yet show the original idea of the chapel, and preserve an interesting monument, unique in the history of art in Scotland, would be an easy matter, if there be the will.

The canopies are still unbroken, and in the chapel. The ambone still exists, Mr Robertson, the present head of H.M. Office of Works in Scotland, having discovered it in a vault below the Parliament House. Soon after the dismantling of the old library I saw the ambone and part of the carved gallery in Mr Matheson's room at H.M. Office of Works. He told me that he had been going over Marischal College Buildings and found the oak tossing about in a lumber room—probably removed for safety from the confusion existing at King's College at the time, in connection with the transference of the books from the nave of the chapel to the new buildings, and he added, "I said to the person with me, a lumber room is no place to leave such work, and ordered it to be sent to the Office of Works." Mr Kerr, shortly before his death, told me that the missing part of the gallery never was in the Office of Works.

---

[1] No doubt the missing part of the gallery is very effective over some sideboard or over a chimneypiece.

[2] Billings, vol. i. No. 7. A drawing of a portion of it, the door of which is singularly like the door of the choir screen of King's College Chapel, has been kindly sent me by Mr Robertson, architect, Dundee, who is engaged in restoring Fowlis Easter Church.

The portion of the carved gallery carried to Edinburgh is now in the chapel. It can be replaced in its original position, and affords a model for reproducing the remainder, if it be not restored. The spirit of reverence must be weak in Aberdeen, or a notice that it is proposed to restore the jube would make the possessor of the missing portion eager to give it back.

What the old position was of each one of the various parts of the screen is not open to question. The continuous notices of the Chapel from 1638 already quoted, and lastly that of Douglas, who tells the number of feet and even inches that the gallery was above the floor (14 feet 4 inches), bring this history far within the memory of those I have talked to, and there are hundreds alive who remember the whole of it, still in the library, as Douglas saw it, and as I have endeavoured to reproduce it from notes I took some forty years ago, standing on the stairs leading to the galleries, shown in Mr Billing's sketch, from which last I have endeavoured to suggest the modern balustrade so much admired by Douglas (Plate LXIII.). I have tried also to have effect given to a strange peculiarity of the roof. On each side of each rib, and round all the bosses and leaves planted on the roof, was a border of black paint about 2 inches broad. In 1823 much of the choir roof was renewed, and in various places where this was done the new carving was not so rich as what remained of the old.

The only room for uncertainty is as to how the canopies, being where we know they were, were originally supported. I can speak to nothing of my own personal knowledge, except the great beam attached to the central canopy. As to the side canopies, the means by which they were supported were more matter of speculation till the partition behind them was removed. Of what was then discovered, I speak from what I was told by the late Mr Andrew Kerr, F.S.A. Scot., an architect of no inconsiderable learning, and a well-known member of the Society of Antiquaries of Scotland.

He was one of the staff in H.M. Office of Works, and went to Aberdeen to inspect the works in the Chapel. He told me that he found on the floor all the old wood that had been found behind the bookcases, much oak and also pine, that though much decayed he had no difficulty whatever in piecing the oak together and seeing that each side canopy was supported by seven uprights of oak, leaving six open spaces, that the upper ends of the uprights were grooved on both sides, and from the analogy of the manner in which the rest of the carving in the Chapel is fixed in position, he believed these

ARCH. SCOT. VOL. V   PL. XXIX

grooves must have been made to receive carved tracery, and he pointed to the choir door as suggesting a probable mode of treatment.

Intending to put nothing by way of illustration of this paper for which I had not absolute warrant, when giving instructions for the preparation of Plates LVII. and LXI., I directed that the side canopies should be supported by simple uprights. But I had mentioned Mr Kerr's opinion to the draughtsman who drew the sketches and he inserted carving between the spars. I was so much struck with its happy effect that I did not have it obliterated. The idea is not mine. It was the deliberate opinion of Mr Kerr.

As regards the central space where the altar was and the crucifix with the Virgin and St John, the canopy over them was certainly attached to the beam stretching across the Church. It must have had support also from the uprights supporting the side canopies, and no further support would have been necessary. Mr Kerr said that the whole space under the central canopy had been found backed with plain oak panellings without ornament. I think it may be assumed that, had the panelling been there originally, it would have been the most richly ornamented of all the rich oak in the Chapel. Farther, it was not usual to have roods so backed. The plain panelling spoken of by Mr Kerr may nevertheless have been from 250 to 300 years old. The College was attacked by the mob from the Mearns in 1569. In 1640 nothing offensive to the Reformers was found in the Chapel except the portrait of the Virgin upon the organ. After the warning of the attack in 1569, it is highly probable that the crucifix and all the statues and plate were removed for safety, and the oak panelling then inserted by the College authorities,—indeed, Principal Anderson was accused of putting church furnishings out of the way.

So much for the **History of what remains of** Elphinstone's College.

The history of the University buildings as a whole would tell a wider story of the history of university education.

Jamieson's sketch (Plate LXV.) gives the original fabric, as completed by Bishop Dunbar, destined for the accommodation of both teachers and taught, for all but two or three of the teachers, who had duties (ecclesiastical or civil) outside, had to live within the walls.

We know that the Principal's chambers were adorned with beautifully carved wainscot within, and the wall "well adorned with several paintings;"

and that of the Chapter house, it was said "ther parlour is fair and bewtiful within." Pococke tells us they had "a very handsome Hall where the students eat who live all in the College." It was 90 feet long, including the vestibule or "lobby,"—"invidenda regibus."

We gather from the repairs ordered in the seventeenth century[1] that besides the south window shown in Plate LXVI. there were three large windows, one at least of which was mullioned and looked to the "wast," "at the heid of the buird"; probably the other two also looked west into the court. There was also a "degrie" (dais?) "at the heid of the Hall buird." There were also seats with backs probably of oak along the walls. There were "two folding tables for the masters and gentlemen's sons to dine and sup at; and six long old-fashioned tables for the use of the bursars to dine and sup at." But lest the large party should be too much given to revelry at their meals there was "in the said common hall a large and high pulpit of wainscot for one of the bursars to read Church History at the time of dinner and supper; and when dinner and supper are ended he reads a chapter of the Bible and sings some part of a Psalm."[2]

Its walls were hung with a selection of ancient worthies connected with the University enumerated by Orem—Elphinstone, Dunbar, Lesley, Scougall, and others. But in his list does not appear Hector Boece, the first principal, nor is he mentioned by Pennant as among the worthies in the hall, nor by Dr Johnson, though we have seen his portrait engraved "from the original in the hall of the King's College, Aberdeen." My father told me that this original (?) was first hung in the hall in the present century, that one of his colleagues, I rather think Professor Duncan, who died about 1820, having been up in London, brought with him on his return this picture, which none of the Senatus could discover any reason for supposing to be, what he thought it, a portrait of Boece,—but to please the donor it was allowed to be hung up, and on his death was not removed. It is gradually acquiring a repute of genuineness from the assiduity with which it has been engraved, and titled as "from the original in King's College."

The oak roof, alcoved like that of the chapel, though different in pattern and with a double row of pendants from end to end, still existed in the first quarter of the present century,[3] but in an utterly decayed state, rendering its removal necessary, as there were no funds for repairing it.

---

[1] *Fasti Aberd.*, p. 282.   [2] Orem, p. 182.   [3] Kennedy, vol. ii. p. 309.

OVER APSE
KINGS COLLEGE CHAPEL, ABERDEEN

SHIELD OF BISHOP ELPHINSTON
REMOVED FROM HALL IN 1827.

I have in vain endeavoured to obtain any old sketch, however rude, of the old Hall; and of all the oak in which it was so rich, there exists, so far as I can learn, but the one fragment transferred to the Chapel wall (Plate LXX.). Under a canopy of vine leaves, such as is so frequently repeated in the Chapel, we have the founder's arms, and below them the pot of lilies with the three salmon fretwise; but, instead of the formal lilies, as in the rendering of the arms of the burgh of Old Aberdeen on the Cathedral roof, or their somewhat freer treatment on the University seal, we have them in rich blossom, encircling and embracing not only the arms, but the very mitre, of Elphinstone, a conceit[1] no doubt due to the special protection of the Virgin, which, according to Boece, Bishop Elphinstone regarded himself as possessing from his childhood, as well as to the honour in which she was held in the diocesan town. For she had her altar in the Cathedral, if it was not dedicated to her, as were the parish church of S¹ᵃ Maria ad Nives and the college and its chapel.

One symptom of educational change already appeared even in Jamieson's picture, namely, the low buildings in front of the gate, called the Grammar School by Gordon of Rothiemay. The "grammaticus" had to teach outside when people not members of the College body applied for education; and when teaching the elements of Latin grammar was discontinued, he still taught in a room adjoining his manse. The gateway of the old manse, with a niche over it containing Elphinstone's shield and mitre, are still visible.

That portion of Gordon of Rothiemay's view, which is given in Plate LV., shows us another stage of the history. There was an influx of students whom the old buildings could no longer contain; so in 1658 the "new wark" of Gordon's day, the "square work" of later days, was built, six stories high, consisting of students' "chambers, a school," a lecture room, "and a billiard house," *mirabile dictu!* Orem, the only authority[2] for this statement, died soon after 1725, so he must have been familiar with the fact. The introduction of this "most gentile, cleanly, and ingenious game" as an amusement for Scots students at that date is surely a very remarkable circumstance. The game is said not to have been introduced into France till the time of Louis XIV.; but must have been very common in England, for Shakespeare makes Cleopatra say, "Let 's to billiards." Probably the

---

[1] The same conceit may be seen differently treated on a shield over the door that led to the chapter house. [2] Except A. Robertson, in 1760, who probably quoted from a MS. of Orem.

suggestion may have been due to some of the English officers then at Aberdeen, who are said to have taken **some interest in** the building the square work. The names of "the Lord General George Moncke" and other officers appear in the list of benefactors in the *Fasti*. This building has come within the last few years to be called Cromwell's Tower, a name I had never heard given to it, but which will no doubt soon become as authentic as the **portrait of Boece!**

The continuing increase of students had led to the necessity for still further accommodation, and Bishop Dunbar's buildings on the south side of the quadrangle, which are written of as much dilapidated, gave place in 1725 to the loftier south side shown (Plate LXVI. fig. 3), erected in **Dr Fraser's** time, and in **no** small degree, like his library, at his expense, and of freestone, taken from the ruins of the cathedral (the central spire of which had fallen) and of the bishop's palace. **On the south side of the quadrangle was a** cloister, where in **stormy** weather the **students in snow and rain might be seen en** *masse* safely walking and taking exercise in comfort, before entering their class-rooms. The cloister was of square pillars, with round arches, and the building was thoroughly uninteresting. The West "Capitol," as it was called in Gordon's time, and the part of the west front shown in Smith's sketch, stood spireless and unused, if not absolutely roofless, till 1825, when it was pulled down to make room for **the present** west front from the design of Mr Simpson, an Aberdeen architect **of some** genius;—considering the state of Gothic architecture at **the time, a clever** solution of the problem of planning what would balance and not be out of **harmony** with the grand old tower and west **end of the chapel (Plate LV.).**

The **view from the** south (Plate LXVI.) shows the mass of the building of 1725 as well as the south end of that of 1825, while in the distance are **seen the** twin spires of the Cathedral, to the enlightenment and liberality **of whose** bishops the College owed its existence, while it formed the brightest **jewel in their mitres.**

To the east may be observed the low humble house of the "Oeconomus," in which I remember the great arched chimney, not of the original kitchen, but of that which replaced it after the numbers to be fed increased on the building of the "square work." **In the** court between it and the Hall was a draw-well, and in it an eel—no one could say how **old!** This view, however, notwithstanding these traces of olden times, shows signs of the growth of the demand for improved teaching accommodation. The six stories of students' chambers in the "square work" are seen reduced to three stories of lecture-rooms. At the date when the sketch was taken, about 1850, no students lived within walls, and I have no recollection of more than two or three at any time doing so. One of the Regents, however, still lived in the Quadrangle. Two had been provided for outside about 1773. The Grammarian had lived outside for centuries, so did the Mediciner, and the old manse of the Canonist had long been allotted to the Sub-Principal. The old Mediciner's manse I remember. It was taken down about 1840; and the Canonist's, attached to the office of Sub-Principal, was replaced by a modern residence after my father's death. Nothing now remains of Elphinstone's extra-mural college buildings but the old gateway with the shield and mitre, from which the old manse of the Grammarian derived its popular name of "The sign of the mitre."

The last view shows the complete transformation of the building in which teachers and taught had lived as one family. Now the accommodation for professors and students alike has disappeared. No one resides in the College, and there is no hall to dine in. The "Oeconomus" and his kitchen, the draw-well and its eel, are no more. Everything but the Chapel, the Crown Tower, and the small Ivy Tower, has been swept away to make room for new class-rooms, and no better can be found anywhere; and the constantly growing library, treble the size of the old one, is seen extending to the east of the old quadrangle, doubling its southern frontage.

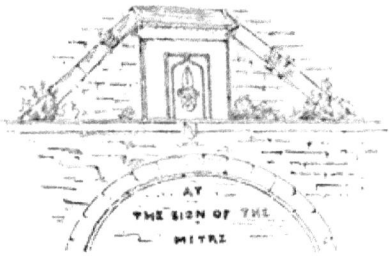

www.ingramcontent.com/pod-product-compliance
Lightning Source LLC
Chambersburg PA
CBHW020240090426
42735CB00010B/1774